Thoughts on Dignity

Ingrid Lindemann

Thoughts on Dignity

Ingrid Lindemann

Impressum

Bibliografische Information der Deutschen Nationalbibliothek:
Die Deutsche Nationalbibliothek verzeichnet diese Publikation in der
Deutschen Nationalbibliografie; detaillierte bibliografische Daten sind im
Internet über http://dnb.dnb.de abrufbar.

Herstellung und Verlag: BoD – Books on Demand, Norderstedt

ISBN: 978-3-7578-8920-3

Prologue

Dear Reader,

This brochure is a short introduction to the WFWP[1]Europe Project "Dignity of Woman". The reader will find a few basic thoughts on the topic and a description of the development of the project.

If this booklet has awakened your interest, I am happy to help you with information and materials, as well as with essays or presentations tailored to your particular situation.

I will also be happy to provide you with the authors and titles of books and essays that have helped us in our research and have provided scientific support for our experiences and findings.

In this case, please contact the organisers of the conference or ingridlindemann@gmail.com

Also, any suggestion or comment is welcome. Please keep in mind that each article in this brochure is only an excerpt from a longer presentation on the subject.

With the wish that this project may contribute to the shaping of a world of peace, I place this short version in your hands,

Ingrid Lindemann

Author and Co-founder of WFWP Europe Project "Dignity of Woman"

---

[1] Women`s Federation for World Peace

Content of this brochure

- ❖ Introduction to the project "Dignity of Woman"
- ❖ Why do we only talk about the dignity of women?
- ❖ What is the meaning of Dignity?
- ❖ Dignity of women throughout the ages
- ❖ Feminine Qualities
- ❖ Dignity and Peace
- ❖ What can I do to strengthen my Dignity-Self?
- ❖ The campaign and project "Dignity of Women"
- ❖ Conclusion: Living dignity is living love
- ❖ Thank you

Introduction to the Project "Dignity of Women"

Women all over the world awaken to their responsibility. Many women are active in the NGOs and politics. In the declaration from UNESCO on the contribution of women to a Culture of Peace we read: "Only as women and men together in equality and partnership can we overcome the difficulties, silence and desperation and secure the understanding, political will, creative thinking and concrete activities which are necessary for global transition from a culture of violence to a Culture of Peace."

One of the eight main goals of the Millennium Declaration in 2000 is to promote gender equality and empower women. (Goal Number 3) Empowering women needs different approaches according to the society, the religious, cultural, and racial background, and the development of the country where they are living. Therefore, we need to meet their needs accordingly. In some developing countries first women need to receive the basic nutrition, education, financial support, and health care.

The Women's Movement in Europe and the USA was successful in many areas. Just think about the right to vote, the right to education, equality and to employment. We can see that there are women today in responsible positions, even as heads of state.

However, are you aware of the fact that violence towards women up to today constitutes by far the most frequent violation of human rights? An issue many times being ignored – yet, since decades governmental and religious institutions provide special homes for battered women and children as refuge from the dangers of violence, sexual intimidation, and physical and psychological abuse. Even on a private level these are criminal acts, oftentimes not recorded due to the economic dependence of women from their partners. This sex-oriented, domestic violence is closely connected with lack of respect towards women and missing of equality of women and men in the awareness of society. Through sexualized language and advertisements, through misuse of the female body as advert-gag for the greatest variety of products, this lacking equality is being reinforced and encouraged very subtle and thus, not only the domestic violence against women but also the abuse of children.

Faced with the continuous degradation of women in many areas, such as forced prostitution, pornography, sexualised advertisement, FGM, widow burning, honour killing, rape as part of war strategy despite all laws and governmental controls, one requirement has to be met first – that of discovering, nourishing and valuing dignity within ourselves. This means that we find ourselves at a point where our inner development stands in direct connection with our influence on society. In other words, as soon as we have discovered the dignity within us, we will live it; we will bring dignity to the world. Then, we can support other women to rediscover the value of their original femininity, to connect to their original mind and to gain the strength to live their dignity and to reject whatever misuses them as women.

Why do we only talk about the dignity of women?

Why do we not talk about the dignity of men? Some men may think, what do I have to do with the dignity of women? But don't you also have a mother, perhaps daughters or a partner? Don't you work together with women in your business? Do you not meet a woman at the checkout in your supermarket, a medical-technical assistant in your doctor's office, a female doctor or X-ray assistant during an examination? Isn't your environment also full of women?

We believe, that when we women find and live our dignity, our husbands, children, fathers, friends, in short, all those around us, benefit from it.

Also, femininity is an inherent trait of all human beings, men, and women alike. If we dignify femininity, we also dignify both man and woman and both find their dignity.

Meanwhile all our lectures can benefit both, men, and women alike. Both suffer from the consequences of lack of awareness of human dignity and the non-observance of human rights in many different aspects.

We start from our personal change. We do not accuse or condemn. We seek the dignity within us to make it the cornerstone of a culture of peace, a culture we all long for.

What is the meaning of dignity?

12

Let us reflect on the meaning of dignity. There are different ways of approaching this topic.

First, let us look at this term very briefly from a historical/philosophical point of view.

Brandhorst[2] outlines 6 periods from a philosophical perspective: Ancient time, Christianity, the Middle Ages, the Renaissance, Modernity, and the period after 1945.

In ancient times, dignity was known only as "official dignity", i.e., privileges and expectations associated with a social position. This then evolved into human dignity based on reason, in conjunction with propriety and self-control.

Through the teachings of Christianity, in which man was understood as the image of God, the idea of fundamental human equality developed. This also demanded respect for the dignity of other people.

In the Middle Ages, dignity was increasingly related to the virtue of the individual. Thus, through "non-virtuous, sinful" behaviour one could also lose dignity and thus all protection. Please recall the horrors of the witch burnings.

In the Renaissance, freedom of the will became the main aspect of dignity. One of the first to have formulated the term 'dignity of the

---

[2] Dr Mario Brandhorst: On the historicity of human dignity, paper presented at Leibniz Uni Hannover, lecture workshop "Human Dignity - Dimensions of its Contingency" Georg-August University Göttingen Lichtenberg-Kolleg 4 October 2013

human being' was a Renaissance-philosopher, Pico della Mirandola In his speech 'De hominis dignitate' (Latin, translation: "About the dignity of the human being") (1486/87), he exposes that man is free to determine his nature in accordance with his own will. He emphasized man's freedom and God given ability to rise to the vision of the deepest secrets of the universe. Literally, he says: 'what an enormous and admirable happiness of the human being, to whom it is given to have what he desires and to be what he wishes to be'.

The philosopher Immanuel Kant[3] spoke of the universal dignity within each human being. He said: "Each person honours the human dignity through his/her own person; has the right to receive respect from others, for the said human dignity; and is in turn, obliged to respect the human dignity in those nearest to him...'

Dignity is within us from the very beginning of life. The neurobiologist Gerald Hüther [4] describes dignity as a neurobiologically anchored inner compass already laid down in the womb that enables people to find their way in the diverse demands of our complex world. New-borns have this inherent dignity as protection and later as compass for understanding what it means to be a human being. Given a good environment this inner compass can later grow and turn to awareness of the internal dignity of this person. No matter what happened in our life or what we did, no matter how much our dignity was hurt, Dignity is within us and can be awakened at any time. Dignity is our internal

---

[3] Immanuel Kant was a German philosopher of the Enlightenment. Kant is one of the most important representatives of Western philosophy. His work Critique of Pure Reason marks a turning point in the history of philosophy and the beginning of modern philosophy.
Born: 22 April 1724, Königsberg
Deceased: 12 February 1804, Königsberg (Wikipedia)
[4] Gerald Hüther "Dignity - What makes us strong as individuals and as a society".

compass helping us in a world of high demands and pressure to keep our identity as human beings, to know our worthiness.

Therefore, it is important to grant dignity first to myself and to be free of any doubt concerning it. Dignity is an immanent nature, an innate character of humans, independent from any other characteristics such as age, intelligence, abilities, and sex.

There are two definitions of dignity which complement each other: Dignity as an essential characteristic and dignity as a mandate addressed to the individual and to society.

Dignity as essential characteristic we find in the Declaration of Human Rights: - "All human beings are born free and equal in dignity and rights."

I want to briefly remind us of the importance given to human dignity in the Human Rights Charter.

 In the Preamble we read:

• Whereas recognition of the inherent dignity and of the equal inalienable rights of all members of the human family is the foundation of freedom, justice and peace in the world …,

• Whereas the peoples of the United Nations have in the Charter reaffirmed their faith in fundamental human rights, in the dignity and worth of the human person and in the equal rights of men and women and have determined to promote social progress and better standards of life in larger freedom.

 In the Resolution 217A (III) of Dec. 10th, 1948, General Assembly of the United Nations we read:

- Article 1 All human beings are born free and equal in dignity and rights. They are endowed with reason and conscience and should act towards one another in a spirit of brotherhood.

Dignity as a mandate is the idea of ethical autonomy of people as we find in the Enlightenment and in the philosophy of Kant. Dignity as a mandate can be directed to the individual as well as to society.

Thus, dignity is defined as our inalienable value as human being. We express our dignity by giving dignity to others. Dignity can only become alive in the relation of giving and receiving dignity.

Let us summarize:

1. Dignity is a human right of everybody. It is your and our inalienable value as human being.

2. Dignity is inherent to us, part of us as our internal compass giving us orientation and helping us to keep our identity, remembering our value and making decisions.

3. Dignity is a way of life. We honour our dignity by giving dignity to others. Dignity can only become alive in the relation of giving and receiving dignity.

Dignity of women throughout the ages[5]

This is only a brief look into history how the awareness of women's dignity was lost and regained.

The awareness of women's dignity has been lost over a long period in history. History taught at schools begins with the civilization of the Sumerians, Egyptians and Greek. Only little knowledge is conveyed about the previous cultures. There have been hundred thousand of years of Palaeolithic culture centring on women and 8000 years of city cultures based on partnership of men and women with a high developed standard. All signs suggest that this have been peaceful cultures because no weapons and demonstrations of repression, slavery and/or wars were found at archaeological excavations.

These cultures came to an end 2000 BC. The decline of the gynocentric society began with the wave of invasions of Indo-European pastoral tribes who brought with them their gods of war. The core of their system was that the power to take life was higher than the power to give life. Power was synonymous with conquering and destruction. The original meaning of power as the live-giving and nourishing force was forgotten. Women had their decision-making power and spiritual authority taken away from them.

The writing of history by the patriarchal cultures begins. This history is viewed from a clearly androcentric perspective. In the antique world, the beauty of a woman was demonised as dangerous and seductive for

---

[5] This is only a short version of the history of women dignity. In seminars about the Dignity of women historic developments are further discussed according to the cultural and religious background of the specific region.

men. Some Greek philosophers claimed that only men were complete human beings.

Around the beginning of the Common Era a movement began, inspired by the teachings of Jesus Christ, which brought with it the beginnings of equal rights for women. He shocked the religious authorities with his announcement that Jews and Greeks, menials and free persons, men and women are all spiritually equal. In early Christianity women held high management positions. Gatherings often took place in the houses of its female followers. However, Jesus' insight that a new values system which includes female values would lead to fundamental change, could not be accepted in by the authorities of those days. The same happened to the teachings of Mohammed.

The American historian Pierre Crabitès (d. 1943) declared that the Prophet Mohammed was "probably the greatest champion of women's rights the world has ever seen".

In the Journal for religious culture, we read: "If one examines the Qur'an regarding the origin of humanity, one realises that according to the Qur'an there is a single origin: "People, we have created you from a man and a woman and divided you into nations and tribes so that you may know each other better. The most excellent of God's creatures among you is the one who is most afraid of sins " In this Qur'anic verse, both the superiority of a race and that of an individual are negated. Only those who live their lives most according to the precepts of religion are considered the most excellent people in God's eyes. There are other Quranic verses that speak of the equal origin of human beings and emphasise that (at creation) no distinctions are made among them, i.e., all human beings are equal at birth. As a result, we can state that the problems of women are not caused by the teachings, here Islam, but arise from cultural and traditional circumstances."[6]

During the dark centuries of the inquisition the Hammer of Witches or "Malleus maleficarum", from 1487 degraded women into imperfect animals. Sexual lustfulness was only identified with women. Even as late as 1910 Max Funke, a German philosopher, wrote a book in which he wished to prove that women are not human beings.

Fortunately, there were in history also men who defended the dignity and rights of women. In the Middle Ages an outstanding champion of the rights of women was Friedrich von Spee. He fought against the eradication of witches at the risk of his life.

So, what have women themselves done to protect their value and their dignity? In the Christian field there is very clearly a history of feminine theology traditions beginning with the female disciples of Jesus, later the deaconesses and woman preachers in the original Christian congregations followed by the female mystics of the Middle Ages. The Venetian theologian and author Christine de Pizan (1405) wrote in "Book from the City of Women" about this female history of theology. She said the works of women are ladders which lead to Heaven.

Since 19th century especially the women's movement, some aspects of feminism have contributed to regaining the awareness of women's dignity.

Through the different organisations of the Unites Nations, through the work of many NGOs awareness has been created of lack of gender equality, the different problems women have to face to live their lives

---

[6] Journal of Religious Culture Journal für Religionskultur Ed. by Edmund Weber in Association Matthias Benad Institute of Religious Peace Research Goethe-University Frankfurt am Main No.. 112 (2008)

in dignity and the necessity of providing support in many different areas. But still, we have a long way to go.

There have always been great women in history who were a source of hope for others, who pointed out the way to a dignified life and lived it as an example. I wish to thank all of them. It would take too long here to mention them all.

Feminine Qualities

If we want to realize a culture of peace the importance of women´s contribution to our world must be recognized. Women have to be supported and empowered to be aware of their value and importance in all parts of our societies. Peace within our families, societies, countries and worldwide can only become a reality when women´s contributions are valued. Gender equality is, first and foremost, a human right. The Vienna Declaration and Programme of Action (adopted in 1993) stated that the human rights of women and the girl-child are an inalienable, integral and indivisible part of human rights. This equality does not imply sameness. Men and women are seen as having different strengths and abilities that enable them to better fill different roles. Gender equality refers to the equal valuing of the roles of women and men. Many times, this has been misunderstood. There are special feminine and special masculine aspects, both necessary and indispensable for a peaceful world.

Also, feminine and masculine aspects exist in both women and men. Talking about feminine qualities therefore refers to both.

Chris Griscom, a (lady) American author and healer said: "The feminine strives in all ideas, with creative efforts, to find that which is common and to unite, in that it, in the face of resistance, discovers openings and solutions and finds that which binds people together in all ideologies and philosophies. Which perspective would be better suited to research, fashion and realise the opportunity to achieve peace? Who is most suited to achieve peace and to educate the next generation to pursue peace? "

Erich Fromm said: "The principle of motherhood is that of unconditional love. The mother does not love her children because they make her happy but because they are her children (or those of another woman). Thus the love of a mother can also not be gained through "good behaviour" or lost through "bad behaviour". ... A mother's love is grace and mercifulness." This kind of motherliness is part of femininity, no matter if or if not, women are mothers themselves. Thus, the feminine aspect of parenthood is the key to sustainable peace making and keeping.

WFWP want to empower women by creating awareness of our specific feminine qualities and thus strengthen our self-respect and understanding, that without us women, respectively feminine qualities, there can be no peace and no further development in the society and the world.

This empowerment is an internal process. We cannot expect to be respected if we don't respect ourselves. We cannot claim women's right to dignity if we ourselves don't believe in our dignity. We can't create peace if we ourselves don't find ways to create peace in ourselves. Accusations and demands on men are in no way helpful. Naomi Wolf wrote in her book "The Strength of Women ", that she does not consider it meaningful to prioritize powerlessness and victim hood of woman, thus accusing the male sex at the same time of imperiousness and aggressiveness. "No-one is served well by such thinking. I would like to set this direction of feminism against power feminism. Its basis is tolerance and respect for feminine individuality and sees itself as feminism of optimism and strength."

On the 3rd of March 2006 there was a headline in the largest newsmagazine in Germany "The Times[7]" asking: "What is feminine? "The editorial department covered this topic in four different articles and two full pages of pictures.

In summarising, all the interviews exposed some feminine characteristics.

• to put oneself in another person's perspective,

 • to perceive the entire situation of the life of another person

• have a viewpoint including all senses,

• to avoid power struggles,

• to wish for efficient teamwork, harmony, balance, creation of common agreement.

This are only some feminine qualities. As soon as we become aware how precious our feminine qualities are, we will have the courage, to find out more. We will discover our abilities and talents. We need to understand our value. We don´t need to copy men`s way of acting to be respected. No FGM[8] is necessary to make us valuable women. Let us help our sisters to free themselves from these ancient traditions. We are different, because we are women, and we are as valuable,

---

[7] Die Zeit
[8] Female Genital Mutilation

intelligent and important for our environment as men. This awareness we must pass on to all women.

Cherishing and cultivating the feminine qualities is an important milestone on our way to live our dignity.

Dignity and Peace

We have come together motivated by a common desire for a peace which encompasses Europe, the Middle East, and the whole world. Through the many faceted aspects of their work, women in Europe have pioneered a wonderful path to that peace but have however often not been recognized or valued by society. Especially after the war women rebuilt their homes and cities. Many men had died, had been wounded or were being kept as prisoners. Women did and are doing still an incredible job, not only in the Europe after World War 2 but all over the world in countries involved in wars, Civil wars or natural catastrophes.

Who really knows how many NGOs have been inspired and led by women? Even today the input of femininity in all parts of society is not easy or to be taken for granted. Therefore, on March 5th, 2010, the "Women´s charter", a declaration adopted by the European Commission on the occasion of the 2010 International Women's Day, stated in the preamble: "Economic and social cohesion, sustainable growth and competitiveness, and tackling the demographic challenge depend on real equality between women and men." Recognizing that although achievements have been made, they are not yet sufficient to grant real equality, Article 4 stresses the importance of dignity, integrity, and the elimination of gender – based violence. "The full enjoyment of fundamental rights by women and girls is an inalienable, integral, and indivisible part of universal human rights and is essential for the advancement of women and girls, peace, security and development. Gender-based violence, including harmful customary or traditional practices, constitutes a violation of fundamental rights, in particular human dignity.

It is inspiring to hear and read all these statements and they are of great support. However, what does dignity mean to me, to us as women? How does this dignity manifest within us? How can we find a way of relating to our dignity? What does dignity mean in our daily life? How is our role in bringing change in our families and our society enhanced by dignity? We need to think about and discover our unique and precious personality. No matter how the various religions or ideologies have considered women up to now, no matter what our teachers have told us, no matter what the life of our mothers and grandmothers has been like, no matter what the role models were, we need to engage in a paradigm shift, to renew the image of womanhood in ourselves.

Mahatma Gandhi said: ""If you want to change the world you have to be the change you want to see in the world." Let us be aware that as well as woman´s role also man´s role has changed. Also, men need to review the traditional image of manhood. Creating this new anthropology of woman-and manhood will be the crucial alliance for the culture of peace. Now is the time to learn to cherish ourselves, to realise that we possess special values, capabilities, and talents which our society so desperately needs. The world today is seeking for feminine values, and this is seen even in politics, where more and more women are elected or appointed to represent their people. Becoming aware of our specific feminine qualities will strengthen our self-respect and understanding, that without us women, as well as the feminine qualities which men possess, there can be no peace and no further developments in society and the world. As soon as we deeply engraft these wonderful abilities to our consciousness, we will find our dignity.

Envisioning the future of our world therefore includes respecting and protecting human dignity as well as living our dignity. However, living our dignity is more than granting dignity to one another, to all mankind. Living our dignity also includes preventing the no observance of human dignity in our society. Only by living dignity can we generate changes in the role model of women and men and bring changes into families, politics, economics, and all aspects of our life.

Once you start being aware of dignity you will discover something new every day. How then can we strengthen our personal feeling of dignity and live with the awareness of dignity in our daily life?

What can I do to strengthen my Dignity?

Many of us had debasing and degrading experiences in their life and thus our dignity has been buried under lots of pain. If we want to strengthen our dignity the first step is understanding how our inner dignity was hurt during our life. Women, and men as well, may have to deal with physical and verbal violence, humiliation, degradation and/ or with being ignored. We do not want to be reminded of painful experiences but allowing us to feel the pain and reflecting on those past or present situations can be helpful to understand why and how our dignity was hurt. Some of us also may need professional help to deal with the pain and internal injuries, especially in case of physical violence. Thus, we can avoid similar experiences and strengthen our dignity.[9]

How to relate to our personal Dignity?

We need to think about our unique and precious personalities, no matter how ideologies or religions have portrayed women historically. It is the time to learn to cherish ourselves and realise that we possess special values, capabilities and talents which our society desperately needs. Becoming aware of our specific feminine qualities will strengthen our self- respect and understanding, that without women and feminine qualities in men respectively, there can be no peace, and no development in the society and world. As soon as we manage to embrace these qualities within our consciousness, we will find our dignity. The discovery of our qualities and development of our talents requires our concentration and investment.

We are all different individuals with different experiences, backgrounds, and character. Therefore, we all go our own way in this process. However, some steps are important and may be helpful for most of us as milestones on our way to living our dignity.

First, let us give a name to our inherent dignity! It is always easier to relate to someone if we know the name. From now on, referring to our dignity, we will call this inherent nature our Dignity Self. This expression is used by Gabriele Frick Baer and Udo Baer, psychological therapists, and authors of many specialist books. If you cannot relate to this expression, you may use another name. Giving a name is the first step to connect to your Dignity. Our Dignity Self needs all our attention if we want to create a culture of dignity.

---

[9] In our seminars we go deeper into this topic.

Connecting with our Dignity Self and strengthening is a process. It is the process of giving and receiving. It takes time. Time is a gift, and we can make use of this gift. Let us not be impatient with ourselves.

Let us start right now. I would like to ask you to straighten up our body. Push your shoulders back and breeze deeply and slowly a few times. Be aware of how you feel.

The first milestone is perceiving and appreciating our feelings, emotions, thoughts, our pain, our joys, fears, everything we do, and we avoid doing without judging or categorizing. We will realize soon how many emotions and thoughts we repress of different reasons. But all feelings and thoughts belong to us and first need to be appreciated and taken care of. Repressing feelings and thoughts take a lot of energy. Respecting our feelings and thoughts, even though we may not like them, helps us to deal with them and understand why we think or feel something. Sometimes, our Dignity Self tries to get our attention by feelings we do not understand. By communicating with our Dignity Self, we may understand. Later I will talk more about this point.

 The next milestone is respecting ourselves. There are many situations in daily life we may not respect ourselves without even noticing. Please ask yourselves: How do I react if I am completely ignored, if someone is disrespectful or humiliates me? These are common day to day experiences. I give just a few examples: Maybe in a meeting nobody listens to your opinion, maybe a coffee you ordered is cold because the waiter talked a long time to someone else on the way to your table. A few days ago, in a shop a lady loudly told me to let her pass because she wanted to take my place waiting in line.

How do I feel and how do I react? Can I ask for respect in a good and dignified way?

How do you feel if someone treats you as the young girl you once were even though you have accomplished so much in your life?

This brings us to the next milestone I like to mention: **Appreciate all you already have done in your life.** Everyone has incredible achievements. But many times, we are not aware of them. We often think that what we did is not worth being appreciated. We think that we just did what had to be done, nothing special. A few months ago, I talked to my doctor because I felt exhausted, without really understanding why. He asked me: How many children do you have? I did not quite understand why he asked me because our children are all grown up and 4 of the 5 children already have their own families. My doctor knows that so why did he ask me? But he insisted and upon my answer he said: And you do not know why you are exhausted? For me having 5 children and helping them to grow up was never connected with the feeling of exhaustion. I enjoyed every moment with them. I did not think about and appreciate my effort and investment. Many times, when we receive compliments and appreciation, we feel uneasy and not worthy enough. That is a sign that we do not respect our own value, our accomplishments, and efforts.

Sit down in a quiet moment and write down everything you already accomplished in your life and appreciate each effort, whether successful or not.

Another milestone is our feeling of self-worth. This is not being arrogant. It is to be aware of our inherent worthiness as human being. Religions call this our divinity or being God's children. Philosophy calls it human dignity. We usually do not really think about our own value. How do you think about yourself? Mostly we feel that we do not meet standards asked for or we doubt our capabilities, our beauty or wisdom. We define our value through our achievements. Self-worth is not depending on what we know, what we accomplished, what position we have, how much we earn, what car we have or how other think about us. This kind of evaluation of 'who am I' and not recognizing our uniqueness and the inherent nature of dignity is one of the problems why we cannot connect to our Dignity Self. Feeling our self-worth also gives us the capacity of valuing other people, discovering their inherent value. Self-esteem and feeling of self-worth only become alive at eye level with others.

Many times, we even feel guilty if we have been mistreated. This is a further milestone: **Let go of feelings of guilt.** Whatever has happened it was not because of you that you were mistreated. Feelings of guilt leave no room for reflection and healing. They restrict us and put a burden on us. In Buddhism the deep sympathy for us as human beings is a high aim and entails redemption. Feel empathy for yourself!

Jesus told us to love ourselves. (Love your neighbour as you love yourself.) Therefore, another milestone on the way strengthening our Dignity Self is accepting myself daily with unconditional love. Get up each morning, look in the mirror, smile and appreciate your beauty. There is no other person like you. You are unique and special.

If we succeed to accept ourselves, we can **live an authentic life**. We do not need any longer to play roles to hide our personality, to wear a mask. Maybe as a child we tried to be a good girl/boy to be loved. Oftentimes as adults in our jobs we accept difficulties to create a positive image. Maybe in friendships we avoid saying our opinion to not lose a friend. Is this necessary? What is a friendship without being able to say your truth? Can you be happy in a job where you always must ignore your needs? Living authentically is an especially important milestone. A real friendship can deal with emotions and different opinions, a job is only good when your needs are respected. Be yourself, you are special! You are unique!

We all experienced situations when we reached the limit. Exhaustion, stress, sleeplessness, and illness pile up on top of us. Yet, how often do we go beyond these? From my own experience I can say: Too often! Again, and again, we just continue, a small break, maybe a painkiller, and off we go again. The show must go on. We all pay too high a price. What must happen before we will finally listen to our body and say 'no' for once? **Taking care of our body and listening to his needs** is another important milestone on the way to live our Dignity.

Another milestone in strengthening our Dignity Self is **developing a sense of your own needs and learning to say no**. I have still to work on respecting my own limits and communicating them. For me this is the most difficult milestone. But in the process, I learned that saying no to requests I cannot deal with straightens me up. Surprisingly my 'no' is always accepted, mostly even without explanation.

A further milestone is letting go of the fear of failure. Many of us may have received the love they longed for as a child by presenting best results at school. This accompanies us throughout our lifetime. We feel our worth only through presenting best results. But our worthiness is not determined by perfect results. Our worthiness is inherent to us since the beginning of life. Therefore, no failure deprives us of our value. we easily forgive others. Let us also learn to forgive ourselves any mistakes or shortcomings. Only then we can turn the feeling of failure into a learning experience. Always remind yourself: You did the best you could.

Be friendly and polite to yourself

Are you surprised? Well, let us be honest. If we realize that we made a mistake we often scold ourselves. Stupid me! I am a complete failure! I am an idiot! Or you look at the mirror in the morning and think "Oh, I look terrible! "You never would say this to somebody else. Why are you more friendly and polite to others than to yourself? I believe it is important to treat myself well, in all aspects of life. I need to give to myself what I would without any doubt give to others. This is not easy at all; I am still learning. Finally take time and **write down all the special abilities you have**. Do not hesitate, just write. Let your Dignity Self help you.

We can communicate with our Dignity Self. Every time we have to make a decision, we can ask our Dignity Self what would correspond to living a life of dignity. We can always say that we need time to decide. We do not need to answer a request immediately. Then we can think about if what we want to do is respecting our Dignity Self. Is what we are asked to do what we really want to do? Does the request respect our privacy? Is it necessary to be done in the time frame established? Is it for a purpose I support? Can I do what is asked for without an uneasy feeling? Does the request respect or hurt my Dignity Self?

Our Dignity Self tries to get our attention by feelings and thoughts which we sometimes cannot understand at first. There might be some uneasiness after a conversation, a feeling of anger, sadness, frustration, or emptiness. If we try to communicate with our Dignity Self, we may find the reason for these feelings. Maybe our opinion was ignored, or we experienced some subliminal humiliation or degradation.

In the beginning of the process of connecting with and strengthening my Dignity Self we may need something to remind us during our daily life not to forget our Dignity Self. In Germany we say: I make a knot in my handkerchief if we want to remember something. May be a small stone in your pocket, may be a note on your desk, may be a meaningful picture on a shelf can help you to be more aware of your Dignity Self.

Always let us keep our sense of dignity: No matter how others treat us, we should never feel we are a victim. Our inherent dignity is much stronger than any evaluation that anyone else may give us. We often have the tendency to be dependent on the compliments from others. It is natural to receive and give appreciation to each other. But to do something only to receive appreciation is hurting our Dignity Self. We all know women or girls letting themselves be misused by men, hoping to get love in return.

We do not need to be ashamed; **it is our right to be appreciated.** We can learn to become independent of the judgement of others, by constantly affirming ourselves that we have dignity, that we are a human being with unique value.

Did you ever think that your life is a unique work of art?

I did not allow myself to think about this for a long time. Often, we feel that we have not done enough – yes that we have never given enough, no matter how much we gave. Through our activism we shy away, in the end, from our spiritual creativity and our self-development. We ourselves are the ones to shape our lives, thus be co-creators of our own 'me'. Discovery of our qualities, development of our talents requires our total concentration, our investment and every new day is exciting and stimulating. Our life is our uniquely personal artwork.

Time is too short today. Please take what I said as inspiration to find your personal way to find and strengthen your Dignity Self. I only want to mention one more point. Dignity not only refers to me but also to everybody else. That means that **dignity is always a way of living**, by granting dignity to others, by respecting and valuing them, by feeling and expressing empathy. Each of the before mentioned aspects corresponds to our own attitude towards others. Only by combining both we can truly strengthen our Dignity Self

Important is to remind us that one aspect without the other does not strengthen our Dignity Self. One without the other does not work.

Self awareness	Be aware of others
Self esteem	Esteem others
Take yourself seriously	Take others seriously
Self worthiness	Regard others highly
Think of myself, take care of myself	Think of others, help others
Accept myself, feel empathy for myself	Accept others, be empathetic
Be able to say 'no' to requests	Live solidarity
Respect yourself	Respect others
Ask to be heard	Listen to others
Be friendly to yourself	Be friendly to others
Be polite to yourself	Be polite to others

You may want to add more aspects to this list or feel that some are not important for you. This is your personal way in the process of strengthening your Dignity Self.

Once we have good communication with our Dignity Self, all that remains is to discover which strengths, dreams, abilities, and desires are within us. I call this the **exploration of the aim of our soul.** That means to give a deeper meaning to our life, quite apart from the external responsibilities. When embarking on this, it is essential to take time. We will come to a more intimate acquaintance with our Dignity Self. The difference between what helps us and what, on the other hand, hinders us, will be clearer to us. In this process, it is important to recognize that even difficult situations can be of help. Some might be an important indication towards the need for a change in our concepts, or way of thinking not to impede our growth. Many happenings in our life serve our internal purpose, correspond to it and further it, often without us being aware of it.

Right at the earliest stages of living our dignity, we often suffocate our desires and visions with thoughts such as: 'I cannot do this anyway, I don't have time for this, this is not realistic, I am not strong enough for this, nobody would understand this, and nobody would accept this!' In our lives we have experienced so many dismissals, have been hurt so frequently that, unconsciously, this became a part of us. Therefore, we often don't realize the internal aim of our soul. Thus, let us learn to desire. The greatest, internal strength arises out of a personal vision. Visions, clear ideas and wishes will give us courage and help us to overcome any external control. When you make your first step on the way to find your Dignity Self, you will feel support from within and from a small beginning undreamed results can develop. We cannot even imagine what wonderful surprises life has in store for us. There is so much within you that urges to develop. Your Dignity Self wants to become visible.

Dignity as a way of life is a cornerstone for a peaceful society and a peaceful world. I want to create awareness about the importance of living dignity. Let us stand together for a future in dignity for our children and grandchildren. Visions and desires are like a fire within us. Let us keep it alight and let it burn brightly.

The Campaign and Project "Dignity of Women"

The first impulse

A short testimony of the first steps of the project by Ingrid Lindemann, one of the founding members

The project began with an invitation to Hannover. Mrs. Anne Weber asked me to give an introduction about our ideas and actions on women and peace. We met in her living room with a small group of women. It was a nice get-together, and the women present listened with interest. At that time, I had no idea that this meeting would set my life on a new course.

One of the women, Maria[10], was very touched by our efforts and asked us to also take up the issue of sexualised advertising. It was a time when even traditional companies used women's naked bodies as an advertising gimmick for office furniture, mineral water, and cars. Sexualised depictions of women's bodies were on almost all magazine covers and on large posters in public places. Clara Maria had already designed a leaflet herself in which she wrote: "Women are called to be responsible with the beauty of the body...We must find our way back to the actual wonderful indispensable values and abilities of women in our society, as loving mothers, spouses and partners, as valued work colleagues and friends...The norm must again become sexuality as an expression of deep love between spouses.

I asked Maria to write a letter to the editor for the WFWP Germany newsletter. Maria expressed how much this sexualised advertising undermines the dignity of women and degrades them as sex objects.

---

[10] Name changed

She wrote: "What is currently happening in the advertising market with women's bodies and thus with women themselves no longer has anything to do with the equality of women in our society."

A leaflet and first actions

This was the impetus to think about the issue of women's dignity. Together with Mrs. Anne Weber and Mrs. Christine Sato, my long-time companions and friends, we began to do research. Yes, Clara Maria was right. Sexualised advertising was everywhere. We designed a leaflet and a postcard with a predefined text to ask shops to remove sexualised advertising from their posters and catalogues.

Mrs. Anne Weber and a group of women started distributing the leaflets in Hannover and organised a book table. The reaction of the people was overwhelming and inspired us to continue. This was the start of our project "Dignity of Woman". It only takes a spark to get a fire going!

Goal of Campaign

Building upon the remarkable framework of human rights legislation to prevent conflict and promote peace and prosperity among and within nations and--- Knowing that human trafficking, sexual exploitation, domestic violence and all forms of abuse constitute an unacceptable violence against women and children that damages the whole fabric of the society and is irreconcilable with a culture rooted in the dignity and value of the human being,---- ---the goal of the campaign "Dignity of Women" is creating awareness of dignity of woman and thus of human dignity.

Aspects of the Campaign

The "Dignity of Women" project has basically two aspects.

• One is restoring the image of womanhood in society. Our slogan is "Let us awaken human awareness fully to the original value and the original beauty of the woman!"

• The other is inspiring women to feel the beauty and value of true femininity, to discover their immanent, God given dignity and to live it.

¬ Call to action: At first, the Women's Federation for World Peace Europe issued an appeal to both women and men who want to prevent, that under the disguise of increased turnovers through advertisement, not only a product is being advertised but, much more, the dignity of women is being undermined and violated. Leaflets and information materials are distributed in many European countries. Further information material was created and distributed on trafficking and forced prostitution,

¬ Seminars: The Women's Federation Europe organizes ongoing educational seminars - Topics are the understanding of dignity and womanhood, the history of women in Europe, the feminine power, the historical chance of contributing to a culture of peace, reconciliation, women and leadership and feminine values as cornerstone for a peaceful world.

¬ Signature campaigns were organized and brought to the corresponding UN agencies.

• Against the rapes in Bosnia

• Against sex and violence in TV

• For the Dignity of Women

¬ <u>Book tables</u> with information material on prevention of trafficking, forced labour and prostitution through understanding and living dignity are always well received.

¬ <u>Special materials,</u> brochures and leaflets for UN days calling on ending violence against women and children, for the conferences and special seminars are available in different languages.

¬ <u>Websites</u> dedicated to this subject and for this campaign help to create awareness.

¬ <u>Networking:</u> Working together with other NGOs which dedicate their efforts to similar purposes.

¬ <u>Conferences:</u> Several annual conferences of WFWP Europe have been dedicated especially to this topic, inviting Women's Federation for Peace Germany to present the campaign on a European level. Each conference emphasised a different aspect of women's dignity in our society in the context of shaping a culture of peace.

- 2007: Vienna/ Seebenstein, Austria: WFWP Europe launched the Dignity of Women campaign
- 2008: Vienna. The title of the conference was: Promoting human dignity to prevent trafficking and addiction WFWP Europe committee members consider this conference to have been instrumental for the success of bringing the awareness of the 'Dignity' of women and trafficking prevention campaign to assist each European country. 60 international participants representing 11 European countries, as well as Japan, Gabon, Nigeria, Mongolia, China and India attended this and worked on a joint resolution together, committing on practical solutions as
    1. to establish hotlines

2. to offer assistancevictims and to report trafficking.
3. to implement international legal procedures for victims' protection
4. the establishment of a European data base on crime, similar to the Italian model
5. governments to improve living conditions of especially the poor and rural populations.
6. to promote a global awareness about the realities of violence against women and children by civil society actors and the media.
7. to address especially the Diasporas of the countries where victims of human trafficking originate
8. to support governmental and non-governmental organizations who work on creating awareness of potential victims, their families, and local communities in the countries of origin.

- 2009 WFWP annual conference took place in Paris. The title was: Concluding the UNESCO Decade of a Culture of Peace: New Alliances to fulfil MDG 3 This conference was a step forward especially in creating alliances between the participating NGOs. Awareness creating and educational aspects in preventing violence against women and children were the focus.
- 2010: This conference took place in Dresden - Empowering women to form alliances to create a culture of peace, focusing on dignity as a cornerstone for building a culture of peace.
- 2011: Madrid: WFWPEurope presented a lecture on Dignity in human relationships.
- 2012: The conference in Rome delt with Women's Leadership in the Culture of Peace. WFWPEurope focussed on Living and acting in dignity.

¬ As a result of the European conferences, the Dignity of women Campaign was presented in other European countries:

• In Strasbourg, December 2007 during a French German Friendship meeting, the project was presented to the participants.

• WFWP Europe presented the „Dignity of Women" at several events in Maribor, Celje and Ljubljana. 18-20th October 2008

o On a Live talk radio program,

o During a WFWP Slovenia Charity concert in Celje

• On Cyprus an Event on Women's Dignity was held on the 6th of May 2009 in Nicosia with presentations translated into Greek.

Meanwhile the project also has been introduced and carried out not only in many European countries but also in other continents, as in the States, Canada, New Zealand and Russia by the respective WFWP organizations.

¬ The Dignity project also was presented on International Women conferences.

For example, on the Women´s World Conference Madrid, Spain, 2008 and the WORLD CIVIC FORUM May 7, 2009, Seoul, Korea: Role of Higher Education for Civic Enhancement "The Dignity of Women and Social Responsibility".

The previous sections are part of the presentation at the 54. CSW annual conference 2010 parallel event of WFWP International. From 1 to 12 March 2010, the Commission on the Status of Women (CSW) conducted a fifteen-year review of the implementation of the Beijing Declaration and Platform for Action and the outcomes of the twenty-third special session of the General Assembly. The focus was on sharing experiences and best practices in overcoming remaining obstacles and new challenges, including those related to the Millennium Development Goals. The meeting was attended by Member States, representatives of non-governmental organisations and UN agencies. A series of parallel events provided additional opportunities for information sharing and networking.

WFWPI, as an NGO with ECOSOC status at the UN, had the opportunity to organise one of these parallel events. Ingrid Lindemann representing WFWP EUROPE was invited to speak at this event about the Dignity project.

The reaction to WFWP Europe`s presentation was overwhelming. Many women from different countries asked for information material, representatives of the White Cross expressed their gratitude and representatives of NGOs working in the areas of human trafficking and forced prostitution said that our work was a wonderful complement to their outreach. Questions on individual points gave the opportunity to explain in more detail.

Since then, many more seminars on Dignity were held, presentations given in many countries around the world, lately also many presentations online for a broader public through media like Zoom as well as presentations to special audiences, for example doctors and therapists.

Also, the content of the Dignity project has always been and will always be expanded by new insights and orientation to new situations keeping in mind the original goals and the importance of being an important cornerstone for a culture of peace.

Conclusion:

I would like to conclude with some points of the resolutions of the 2009 conference.

Therefore, we commit ourselves to:

- Seek opportunities to mediate, motivate and monitor our governments at the local, national and international level to fulfil the MDG's, the Universal Declaration of Human Rights, SC Resolution 1325 and other commitments in support of the culture of peace,
- Use our influence to teach the value of dignity and appreciation of diversity to our children, through words and actions, from the earliest age, especially as concerns the equal value of women and men.
- Raise public awareness about violence, seeking to involve men and boys in activities for the prevention of violence against women and towards the empowerment of women and girls,
- Take responsibility to solve cycles of enmity by building partnerships and commit together to goals and programs for a common peaceful future,
- Promote civic participation by engaging social and government institutions to include peace and character education components in their programs- formal and non-formal education for peaceful resolution of conflicts, mediation, and reconciliation.
- Promote paradigm changes whereby empowerment comes through cooperation, not confrontation.
- Calling for a code of conduct for a responsible media.
- Engaging youth as co-planners and partners for the continued work towards a culture of peace and prosperity.

- Providing respect and appreciation for our elders that they may "Age in dignity"!

Living Dignity is living love

Only by living dignity can we generate changes in the role model of women and bring changes into families, politics, economics, and all aspects of our life.

Living dignity is accepting each other and recognizing the differences in culture, tradition, religion, and character as enriching.

Living our dignity means overcoming and healing the wounds of past conflicts. WFWP Europe has celebrated Women´s Friendship meetings crossing the Bridge of Peace with women from former enemy countries. These "Bridge of Peace ceremonies" are a foundation for more understanding and appreciation of each other beyond all borders by sharing thoughts, feelings, experiences and finding common interests and solutions to problems in our respective communities.

Living our dignity is giving a new role model to our young people and changing the educational emphasis to living dignity. In July 1997 Nobel Prize winners from all over the world signed a declaration. They wrote:

"The future of the world hangs on our willingness to really change. --We must dare to tell young people, even in history classes, that they will contribute more to the world by living in dignity than by dying heroically, that it is conscience, rather than obedience, which is the basis of human life. The only real challenge remaining today, the real issue which will define the future, is, for the first time, to live together by respecting ourselves, each other and the environment. "

The respect of human dignity is a way of life:

- Living our dignity is meeting one another at eye –level.
- Living our dignity is looking at each other through the eyes of dignity.
- Living our dignity is meeting one another in our common origin, meeting as children of the one God, beyond all religious differences.
- The eyes of dignity do not judge.
  When we meet respecting our dignity, we do not expect the other to be or act as we want, because we can enjoy the variety of all character types.
- Living our dignity is sharing without expecting, giving without asking.
- Respecting our dignity is trusting each other.
- Dignity includes empathy.
- **Living our dignity is living love.**

Thank you!

Dear Reader,

I hope you were able to get an impression about the project and the importance of living dignity.

I am only one of many women who have been shaping this project.

I want to thank each one of the wonderful ladies who have accompanied me and this project over the years. Without them, without the support of WFWP Germany, WFWPEurope and the UN Office of WFWP International this development could not have been possible.

Only together we can create a culture of peace for the next generations to come. Living dignity is one very important cornerstone.

I hope we could inspire you to join us in this effort.

It only takes a spark to get a fire going!

 Yours,

Ingrid Lindemann